A Brief History Of The Town Of Stoneham, Massachusetts: From Its First Settlement To The Year 1813

Silas Dean

A BRIEF

HISTORY

OF THE

TOWN OF

STONEHAM, MASS.,

FROM ITS FIRST SETTLEMENT TO THE YEAR 1843;

WITH

AN ACCOUNT OF THE MURDER OF JACOB GOULD,

On the Evening of Nov. 25, 1801.

BY SILAS DEAN.

PUBLISHED BY REQUEST.

STONEHAM:
SENTINEL PRESS, H. C. GRAY, PRINTER.
1870.

HISTORY, &c.

According to the best information that can be obtained, that tract of land included in what is now called Stoneham, was first settled about the year 1645. In the year 1640, four brothers by the name of Holden, came over to this country from the county of Suffolk, in England. The fifth and youngest brother of the family remained in his native land. Three of the names of those who came to this country were Richard, Oliver, and Justinian. Oliver took up a permanent residence in the vicinity of what is now Charlestown Square. Many of his descendants are still living in that place. Justinian not being able to procure land to his liking, finally removed to what is now the town of Westminster, at the northern part of Worcester County. He took possession of that township, and lived there the remainder of his days. After his decease, a monument was erected to perpetuate his memory, and also stating the facts connected with his settlement in that township. His descendants still remain there, and are among the most wealthy and influential members of society. The fourth brother (whose name is not known) removed to the State of Connecticut, and nothing further is known with regard to him. It will be remembered that this town was at that time (and indeed till the year of its incorporation, which was 1725), a part of Charlestown. Richard it seems concluded to remove to the northerly part of the town. The house which it is said he built and lived in, stood from twenty-five to thirty rods southwest from where the house of Nathan Bucknam now stands, at the southwest part of the town. From Richard Holden it appears all (in this immediate vicinity) of that name descended. Richard Holden's first child (whose name was Samuel,) was born in the year 1649. Asa Holden, now living in this town, is a descendant of Richard, of the fifth generation, Asa Holden's grandfather being a grandson of Richard. I find an ancient stone in the burying yard with the following inscription: "Here lies ye Body of Mrs. Anna

Holden, wife of Samuel Holden, who departed this life June 18th, 1731, aged 72 years." This was evidently the wife of Richard's first son. According to the date of her death, she was born in the year 1659. As I have before stated when the four brothers came to this country, which reason was that they might enjoy their religious sentiments unmolested, that the youngest brother remained in his native land. I am told that the Holden family were heirs to the estate of a rich lord, who was a bachelor. After the decease of this rich lord, the remaining brother took the property which they inherited, and with his family removed to this country, in 1646. He purchased a large tract of land and settled in the State of Rhode Island. He made every effort possible, (as has been since ascertained,) to find his brothers and give them their several portions, but all his efforts proved unavailing, and all his hopes of enjoying his new home and religious privilege, were soon blasted. In a few short months he sickened and died. All hopes of finding his brothers being given up, the disconsolate widow sold his estate, took all the property in her possession, (which no doubt was a very handsome sum,) and returned back to old England. Mr. George Piper, who lived in East Woburn, a few years since, (an Englishman by birth,) stated that he was knowing to a large sum of money being deposited in a certain place near London or Liverpool, by the name of the Holden fund, which gives us reason to suppose that this was the very legacy left to this family; but which, if not called for after a certain length of time, would be appropriated by government, as they saw best.

Some persons have supposed that the first person that took up a residence in town, was a Scotchman named Hay, but if the record kept by Asa Holden be correct, which I cannot doubt, as he has the date of births down to himself, then it is certain that Holden was here previously. Hay was the first at the centre of the town. The circumstances of Hay's coming to this country were as follows: He was bound out as an apprentice in the city of Edinburgh, Scotland, but being dissatisfied with his situation, he resolved on leaving his master. He accordingly took passage for this country on board a vessel bound for Salem. On arriving at Salem, being unable to pay his passage, which must have been considerable at that time, the captain of the vessel sold or bound him out to a man in Lynnfield, to work till he should pay his passage, which was something like six or seven years. After serving out his time he concluded to come into this vicinity and settle down. He commenced his first labors by clearing up the ground about what is now called Cobble Hill. It is stated that he came over from Lynnfield with his axe and gun, stopping for a few days only at a time, and lodging in a building or hut which stood on or near the spot where the house of Reuben Locke, Jr., now stands. It appears that he stood somewhat in fear of the Indians, although he purchased his land of them, at the rate of two coppers per acre.

I shall now give an account of the ancient buildings, together with some incidents connected with the inhabitants who dwelt in them. Richard Holden, it will be remembered, located himself a short distance southwest from Nathan Bucknam's. About twenty rods southwest from his house, another house stood for several years occupied by a family named Howe. About fifteen rods west from Nathan Bucknam's, a house formerly stood owned by Samuel Holden. In this house Asa Holden, now living, was born. It is but a few years since this house was taken down. On the southwest side of Bear Hill, a house stood many years since owned by a man named Spring. The land in that vicinity still retains that name. A little further to the north or northwest there stood a building, as a cellar hole at present shows. Who lived in it, or when it was inhabited is not at present known. Still farther to the north a building stood occupied by a man named Parker. This house was at length removed to the southeast part of the town, was repaired, and occupied by Thomas Vinton, during his lifetime. At the present time occupied by Reuben Waitt. About one hundred rods northwest from Nathan Bucknam's, a house stood many years ago, occupied by a man named Hadley, who married one of Richard Holden's daughters. Anthony Hadley, who died several years since, at an advanced age, is said to have been a member of that family. It may be well to state the circumstances connected with the settlement of the first person by the name of Hadley in this town. A man by the name of Gould, living at or near the place where Thomas Gould now lives, on a certain morning during the first settlement of the town, while at his barn at a very early hour, a man approached him, stark naked, and told him he came over to this country on board a war ship. The night previous he had deserted from the ship, and being fearful that his clothes might retard his escape, or the procuring of them cause some alarm, he left the vessel in a state of nudity. He also stated to Gould that if he would provide him with

clothes, and afford him means for keeping himself secreted
till after the vessel left Boston, he would work for him a
sufficient length of time to satisfy him for all the trouble he
might be at. The proposal was agreed to, and by this means
Hadley took up his abode in this town, and from him all of
that name now living in town descended.

Richard Holden's farm originally included the land owned
by Spring, Parker, Howe, and Hadley, before mentioned. It
took in the land of Jesse Dike; it also took in the Hill farm,
(the house standing on said farm is at present occupied by
A. C. Butterfield and Benjamin Wheeler, and is owned by
Warren Sweetser,) and the two farms of Messrs. Chamber-
lain and Hackett, situated in Woburn.

The House of Jesse Dike is said to have been built by a
man named Hadley. It was afterwards occupied by the
father of Capt. James Steele. A few rods northwest from
said Dike's house, there stood a building owned by a Mr.
Knight, a tailor by trade. Richard Holden's land is supposed
to have extended as far north as where the saw mill owned
by David H. Burnham now stands. On this water privilege
there formerly stood a grist mill. I am told that a deserter
from some war vessel had secreted himself under the floor
of this mill. The British soldiers, who were sent to take
him entered this mill. It seems they were pretty well satisfied that he was there concealed. They walked the floor,
stamped, being enraged no doubt, while he was protected
from their vengeance by only the thickness of the board or
plank of which the floor was made. He, however, providen-
tially eluded their grasp. A house stood near the mill occupied for many years by a man named Gould. An old fire-
place was dug up there a few years since while preparations
were making for the laying of a wall.

At the north of this, the Scotchman Hay is said to have
been owner of the lands. He probably owned as far north
as where the school-house in District No. 1 now stands. At
the north of Scotchman Hay's, a man named Gerry
owned the lands. The circumstances of his coming to this
country are as follows: He came over in a man-of-war, acting in the capacity of a boatswain. At Boston he fell in
company with Hay, came out and surveyed the land; being
pleased with the prospects of taking up his residence here,
he returned to Boston, got permission to return here and
live, with the promise that if ever called for to go on an ex-
pedition against the enemy, (French) he must go. To this
Gerry consented. The house in which he lived stood a few

rods north from the house of Benjamin Gerry. He became acquainted with a young lady in Boston, whom he married and brought to this place. Gerry is said to have been a man of great courage. The following incident will prove it to be the fact. At that time this country was inhabited to a considerable extent by wolves. On a certain day, Gerry was out either for labor or business. He called upon a family, living upon or near where the Almshouse now stands, about dusk. It was thought rather dangerous for him to return home; however, having an axe with him, he proceeded homeward, but before proceeding far, he came in contact with a number of wolves. He braced himself against a large tree and ptiched battle with his antagonists. The neighbors heard the conflict, notwithstanding he was left to conquer or die. He conquered, and returned home. In the morning he went to the place where he fought, and there found that he had killed no less than four wolves, the fifth had walked off, leaving blood to show that he also had been wounded. The bounty on wolves was at that time about £4 each. Gerry remained here for many years, but was called upon to fulfill his engagements, made previously to settling here. He left his wife and children, never to return; as it is said he fell during an engagement with a foreign enemy. He had several sons. One settled in this town, another went to Harvard, and another to Marblehead. Elbridge Gerry, formerly governor of this State, and vice-president under Mr. Madison's administration, is said to have been a member of this family.

The house now owned and occupied by Capt. Rufus Richardson, was built many years ago, and formerly owned by a man named Wiley; afterwards occupied by the father of Benjamin Gerry. The house owned by Elijah Richardson was formerly known as the Matthews place. It is thought to have been built about seventy years since. An ancient building formerly stood a few rods to the northeast of this; and for a considerable length of time was supposed to be haunted. A family lived there at that time. At the season of harvesting a quantity of pumpkins were carried into the garret; one evening while the father was absent, and the mother with the children and other members of the family sat by the fireside, a noise was heard; something appeared to be coming down stairs. It came stamp, stamp, down the garret stairs; it then came to the entry stairs, which led to the lower door, and with increased force, came pound, pound, into the entry below. There the noise ceased. The affrighted family waited with great anxiety for the return of the husband and father. When he returned the news was communicated to him. He repaired to the entry, when on opening the door a good lusty pumpkin was reposing on the floor. Whether the house was ever afterwards haunted, is not known. The house of Oliver Richardson has also been built for seventy or eighty years. A few rods to the northeast there formerly stood an ancient building occupied by the father of Oliver Richardson. I am told he kept bachelor's hall for many years. Something like seventy or eighty rods northeast from this, a cellar hole shows that a building once stood there; and still further to the north, on the north side of the road leading from the house of Caleb Wiley to Mr. Leathe's, in Woburn, there stood an ancient building called the old Farm House. For some length of time a negrc named Simon Barjona, lived in the house. He was a shoemaker by trade, and Mr. Elijah Leathe, who was a neighbor to him, sometimes employed him to make shoes for him. On one occasion Mr. Leathe purchased a side of upper leather and also a side of sole leather; he carried them to Simon, requesting him to make him a pair of shoes. The shoes were made to order. Mr. Leathe did not take home his leather with him, but left it till he should want another pair of shoes made. When his family were again in want of more shoes, he repaired to Simon, told him he wished for a pair, stating the size, &c. Simon immediately replied that he had no ludder. No leather, says Mr. Leathe, why, did I not leave leather with you. Simon immediately replied, O yes, massa Leathe, but ludder no hold out. The fact was he had shod his children from time to time as they needed; to be sure the ludder had held out pretty well for Simon, but it fell short indeed as far as Mr. Leathe was concerned. Simon had several children; I see the record of three baptized by Rev. Mr. Carnes, second minister in this town, viz: Abigail, Hannah, and Isaiah. His wife's name was Hannah. She was frequently called old Hannah Qut. She is said to have been part Mulatto and part Indian blood. Simon was purely negro, I believe; though it is stated that his wife said on a certain occasion that he was nothing but a brown Englishman.

The house occupied by Caleb Wiley has been built for many years. An ancient building formerly stood a short distance to the northeast, occupied by a family said to have been murdered by the Indians. The inhabitants were alarmed immediately after the murder, and repaired to th house; being armed, they proceeded in search of the murderers; about one-third of a mile west from the house of Caleb Wiley, they discovered an Indian near a rock; they fired upon and killed him; they also found seven packs near him, from which circumstance it is supposed that six more were in company with him. An old building formerly stood a few rods east of the house now owned and occupied by Widow Mirandi Richardson. The year when it was built is not known. An ancient building also stood on the spot where the house of Ephraim Pierce now stands. In this building the father of Mr. Pierce lived many years. The mother of Mr. Pierce, it will be remembered, was formerly the wife of Mr. Ashael Porter, of Woburn. On the morning of the ever memorable 19th of April, 1775, he was desired by a neighbor, Josiah Richardson, to proceed with him towards Lexington (about three o'clock, A. M.). Somewhere on the way they discovered some British Regulars. Porter and Richardson were also seen by the Regulars, and were taken by them. Richardson requested permission to return, and was told by the individual to go to another person, who would no doubt give him a release; but in case the second person he went to told him to run he was by the first ordered not to run; being informed that if he did run he would be shot. Richardson did as he was told to do; and though he was told to run, he walked away, and was not injured. The reason why he was ordered to run was this: that the guard might think him a deserter, and thereby, in the discharge of their duty, shoot him. Mr. Porter not being apprised of their artifice in telling him to run, got permission in the same way of Richardson. Having liberty to go, he set out upon the run. On getting over a wall a short distance off, he was fired upon and received his death wound. His bones now lie in Lexington with the seven who fell on that morning, while defending their rights as freemen.

The old building now owned by Elias P. Bryant, and occupied by Phineas Green, was formerly owned by Nathan Simonds. When it was built is not at present known. The old building which stood something like sixty rods south from Benjamin Gerry's, was occupied for many years by David Gerry. It was burnt down about twelve years since.

On the top of Farm Hill, at the northwest corner of the land now owned and improved by B. F. Richardson and B. F. Tay, there stood a building many years ago, occupied by a man named Grover Scollay. A rock near that place, is at present called Scollay's rock; from the fact, it is said, of

Scollay's being in the habit of going out early in the morning and sitting upon it, whether for the purpose of meditation or to view the surrounding scenery, I cannot tell.

The building which goes by the name of the Old Office, has been standing for a great number of years. How it received its present name is not known; but if the receiving and drinking of rum within its walls, in by-gone days, could give it this title, it has surely, with great propriety, been conferred upon it. The house in which Capt. David Hay kept tavern for many years, and also his successor, David H. Burnham, is one of the oldest buildings in town. Capt. Hay for many years had a negro servant named Daniel Kingstone. When slavery was abolished in this State, Kingstone was set at liberty, with the rest; but unlike some of his southern brethern, who take their liberty without permission, he chose to spend the remnant of his days with his old master. The house now occupied by John Wheeler, and owned by Dea. Reuben Richardson, was built about the year 1776, by Mr. Thomas Fosdick, of Charlestown. The house occupied by the widow of the late Capt. Jonathan Hay, was built in the year 1725. The bricks used in building this house were drawn over the eastern ridge of Farm Hill, as a road led that way previous to the building of the turnpike, which was about thirty-eight years since. In the house before spoken of the old Scotchman, Hay, breathed his last. The building he lived in previous to this stood a few rods to the south. He died in 1748, being in the 91st year of his age.

During his life time he is said to have married no less than five wives. At the last marriage ceremony, (which took place after he was seventy years old,) he is said to have displayed his youthful buoyancy, by dancing on the occasion. About a quarter of a mile east from the house of Widow Hay, on the road leading to South Reading, a house once stood, occupied by a man named Damon, who was a blacksmith and shovel maker by trade. The house occupied by Walter Blaisdell, (known as the Hay Place,) has been built about thirty-eight years. The building owned by the town, and used as an almshouse, has been standing for a great number of years; it was formerly owned by Mr. John Cutler. Mrs. Cutler, who outlived her husband by several years, bequeathed to the church the sum of one hundred dollars, the interest only to be spent annually for the benefit of the needy members of the church. The house of John Jenkins, is an ancient building, and probably has stood for more than a hundred years.

The house of the late Daniel Gould, Esq., has been built for many years; though from its external appearance, having been many times repaired, one would suppose that it was not of long standing. An old building formerly stood where the house of Capt. Buck now stands, known as the Bryant Place. Mr. William Bryant states that for three or four generations back from his father, one or more of the family were blacksmiths and shovel makers by trade.

Two Scotchmen formerly lived in that section of the town, named Dunton, and Ingerson. Dunton was a trumpeter, and belonged to the troop company then in this vicinity. He is said to have adopted the practice on certain occasions, (when the Indians were committing their depredations in the neighborhood,) of putting his trumpet out at one of the windows of his house and playing, in order to alarm them. A house stood, during the first years of the settlement of the town, on the spot where the house of the late Daniel Gould, Esq., now stands. In this house one of his ancestors lived by the same name, Daniel Gould. He held the office of cornet in the troop company, amounting to about the same as that of ensign in a militia company. On a certain morning, wishing to call the members of the company together for the purpose of going to capture and destroy some Indians, if possible, he discharged the contents of a pistol into the upper part of his house, a wad it is supposed set the building on fire and reduced it to ashes. Several individuals at that period lived in the northeast section of the town, denominated squatters. This name has particular reference to those individuals who in the early history of this country were in the habit of clearing up a small patch of ground where it should convene them. Sometimes they would remain, purchase the land, and also buy several acres adjoining. But they were generally under the necessity of soon leaving their temporary abodes. In a southerly direction from the house of Israel Newhall, there was formerly a tan yard, some remains of which may be seen at the present day. The house of Daniel Green, is one of the oldest buildings in town. This was formerly called the Souther Place.

I find a record made by Rev. James Osgood, first minister of this town, of a church meeting being held at the house of Mr. Souther, Nov. 2d, 1731. The house now owned by the Misses Newhall, was occupied by Rev. Mr. Osgood; when it was built I am unable to say. An ancient building formerly stood a few rods east from the house of William A. Rowe, and was taken down by him in the year 1812. Still farther to the east, he states, a building once stood. This part of the town was settled at an early period. Mr. Rowe states that he found, but a few years since, a living spring of water—with a tub in it; none of the inhabitants knew anything with regard to it. The tub was about four feet from the surface of the ground, and was found in ground previously supposed to be destitute of springs.

An ancient building also stood where the house of Reuben Locke now stands, which was taken down about the year 1820. This house and that of Mr. Jenkins were both built in one year. About fifty rods north from Mr. Locke's a house formerly stood, on what is now called Spring Hill. The name of the man who lived there, is said to have been Kibby. An excellent spring of water on the north side of the hill is called Kibby spring. The house of the late Capt. Daniel Green was built about sixty years since. An ancient building is said to have stood a few rods farther to the east, in which Elder Daniel Green lived the last part of his lifetime, He was elected Elder of the church about the time of the settlement of the Rev. Mr. Carnes, which took place in the year 1746. Elder Green formerly lived in a building which stood a short distance southwest from the house of Joseph Vinton. This building or one standing not far from it, was called the Wilson House, and was afterwards moved and placed upon a cellar a few rods south or southeast from the house of E. H. Stearns; it was taken down by Major Jesse Green, something like thirty years since. The house of Joseph Vinton has been built about fifty-six years. The building formerly standing on this spot was destroyed by fire, The house of Dr. Levi Gould has been built for several years. The building first occupied by the Vintons, stood near this. The house of John and William Green has been built about forty years. Previous to the building of this, an ancient building stood about thirty rods to the northwest, used as a garrison, at the time of the conquest between the first settlers and the Indians. The house occupied by the widow of the late Johathan Green is supposed to have been built about the year 1700. Jonathan Green, who lived in this house was one of the first settlers. When he first moved into this house he used the east part of it for a stable. This man, woman, child and horse, all lodged under the same roof, Green was also a member of the troop company, and often went to Groton and vicinity, as this was a great place for the destruction of the Indians by the early settlers. The house now occupied by Widow Johnson has stood for a great num-

13

ber of years. Also the house occupied by Mr. Holt. This was formerly owned by Mr. Thomas Green, previous to that by a Mr. Knight. In this house a negro named Cato died many years ago. Cato was the son of Simon, a negro servant of Dea. Green. I am told that for some years before his death, he lived during the summer season in the first school-house ever built in town, which stood something like fifteen rods southeast from Jacob Gould's. The house of Nathaniel Stevens was built many years since by a man named John Wright, of Charlestown. A short distance northeast from the house of said Gould a building formerly stood, owned by a man named Phillips, who is said to have been a man of uncommon courage. He was a member of the troop company. While they were on an excursion at a certain time for the purpose of destroying the Indians, somewhere near Concord they came in contact with a company of these sons of the forest, skulking in a rye field. Phillips entered the field with the others; he was cautioned to be on his guard. He immediately answered in his usually decided way, that he was not afraid of the black rogues. Scarcely had the words escaped his lips, ere a musket was discharged. Phillips received a fatal wound, sprung several feet from his horse and expired. The last member of his family is said to have died about twenty years since, in the town of Malden. The house of Samuel Brown is also a relic of antiquity. For many years a tavern was kept there. The house of the late Ebenezer Bucknam is one of the oldest dwellings standing; this was the place of rendezvous during the time of the Revolution. The house occupied by Dea. Jabez Lynde, and James H. Gould, is also a very ancient building. It was formerly owned by a Scotchman named Maize. Maize, as I am informed, came to this country (like many others who settled here) on board a war ship. One night as the vessel lay at anchor somewhere near Boston, Maize resolved to desert. He accordingly bound his clothes to his back, leaped from the vessel, and swam ashore. He came out here and took up his abode. Subsequent to Maize, an Irishman named Toler came in possession of the aforementioned house. He kept a kind of tavern for some time, also selling goods of various descriptions. It is said that previous to coming to this country he had the plague; that he was taken in a very sudden manner. One report is that he dug his own grave and got into it, expecting soon to die, but that the ground had the wonderful efficacy of removing the plague. Another statement made is that the attending physician opened his

scull and inserted a small piece of silver, which produced a
cure. One or more of the reports are no doubt true. It
has also been said that an individual who recovers from
this dreadful disease, will never again be subjected to any
disease, but that such persons will finally die of old age.
This was verified in the case of Toler, who lived to be about
ninety-four years old and at last died in his chair, apparently
as easily as he would have gone to sleep. He had a slave
named Dinah, who waited upon him to the end of his days.

Toler used to teach school in the school-house which stood
north of the town pound, which was the second school-house
built in town. I am told that he was in the habit of send-
ing some scholar to the tavern of James Hay, (which stood
where the shoemaker's shop of Jacob Gould now stands,)
about eleven o'clock in the morning, to get a glass of grog
and carry it to the school room for him to drink. What
would the members of the Cold Water army say, in 1843, if
sent out by their teacher to procure a glass of grog for him?
Methinks they would not only sing "away the bowl," but
with indignation would they sing, "away, away the teacher."

After the death of Toler, Capt. Samuel Ingalls kept tavern
in that house for several years. The sign first stood a few
feet southwest from the house. The sign I am told was
painted by an Indian named Sol. Wamscott. A few rods to
the east from this a house stood many years ago occupied by
a family named Buck.

The house of James Hadley, I am told was built many
years ago by a man named Eben Knight. The house of John
Bucknam I am told was built by a man named Allen. It
has been built for more than a hundred years. An ancient
building formerly stood a short distance south or southwest
from this, occupied also by a man named Allen. The house
of Thomas Gould is a very ancient building. It was standing in 1714. How many years previous to that is not known.
It is probable however, that it has stood nearly one hundred
and fifty years. The house occupied by Timothy Sprague
has been built about sixty years. A short distance southwest from this there stood a building, many years ago, known
as the Guard House. This was built by Timothy Sprague,
that a family might live there and guard the dam, by which he
flowed Spot Pond, as it had been several times taken away. It
appears that several persons in town were opposed to having
Spot Pond meadows flowed; and consequently they had a
good deal of contention with Mr. Sprague at different times.
They frequently went to law, but Sprague was generally

successful in getting the case. At that period, a man by the
name of Jabez Allen lived in town. He is said to have been
a horse thief, and also well skilled in all kinds of roguery.
He was in the habit of going in a boat to the dam, for the
purpose of taking said dam away. He also took his gun with
him. When any person appeared, to drive him from his labor,
he would get into his boat and sail to a small island near by.
On a certain occasion while at work taking away the dam,
Sprague approached him, with orders to desist. He quickly
got into his boat and sailed to the island. His gun being
loaded with buck shot he discharged the contents of it at
Sprague. He was wounded in one or both of his legs. Allen
was prosecuted. What his punishment was at this time I
am not certain. Either at this time or for some other offence
he was sentenced to sit upon the gallows for several hours.
This being as agreeable to him as sitting in a parlor, he occupied his time in making poetry. The following is a speci-
men of it.

> Some call me Jaby Allen,
>   And others they call me Medes,
> And here I sit upon the gallows,
>   For all my evil deeds.
>
> O that I were the judge,
>   Now, in poor Jaby's case;
> I'd have poor Jaby out of jail,
>   And have old Tim Sprague in his place.
>
> Old Cambridge is a mighty place
>   For learning and for knowledge,
> For some they whip, and some they hang,
>   And some they send to College.

Allen at length became so bad to deal with that he was
finally sold on board a man of war. The captain of the vessel having heard of his evil deeds told him on a certain day
that he should like to see some of his iniquitous feats. Allen
with a good deal of apparent sobriety, told him that he was
not in the habit of practicing unlawful deeds. A short time
after, however, Allen got a handsaw and sawed all the oars
on board the vessel nearly in two, with the exception of one
pair. When a convenient opportunity presented itself he
took a small boat and the only pair of oars, (good for any
thing,) and started for the shore. The alarm was soon given
on board, that one had deserted. Orders were immediately
given to have the boats lowered, which was done. The boats
were manned. The oars on being used went crack, crack,
one after the other, till they were all used up. This being
done, they fired upon Allen a few times. This did no good.

Orders were then given to pour a broadside upon him; but he had got so far that it did no good, and thus he effected his escape.

The house owned and occupied by the widow of the late Daniel Bryant, and which was destroyed by fire a few years since, was built in the year 1805.

The old Sprague house, so called, is the last building on the old road to Medford. In this house lived Capt. Samuel Sprague, who commanded the company in this town, during the time of the Revolution.

The eastern section of the house owned by Joseph Hurd, was built about fifty years since by Nathan Willey. The western part of said house was put up by Luther Richardson, Esq., in 1806. The building which goes by the name of Hurd's old factory, was built in the year 1792. It was first used as a snuff mill, afterwards enlarged and used for the purpose of manufacturing satinets. The mill owned by Oliver Wheeler, was built in 1812. It is used for grinding cinnamon, ginger, and various medicinal articles. The house near it was built about the same time. The house occupied by Mr. Baldwin, was built in 1803. The mill near the house is used for the purpose of turning various articles. On this spot (or near to it,) a chocolate mill formerly stood. At the northwest from Mr. Baldwin's, there stood a building many years since occupied by a man named Anthony Hadley. A few rods northeast from Mr. Baldwin's, a house once stood owned by Ebenezer Bucknam.

The house of Asa Holden has been built about one hundred years. A few rods north from this an Irishman with his wife lived, many years since. He finally moved to the northerly side of Doleful Pond (so called), cleared up about a quarter of an acre of ground, and lived the remainder of his days. He died in a very sudden and unexpected manner, at quite an advanced age.

A house formerly stood a few rods southeast from the school-house in District No. 4. This house was occupied by a man named Hadley. The circumstances of his death were as follows: He with his son had been to Medford on some business; he did not return homeward till night. It was a cold, stormy evening, in the last of November or the first of December. On his return home, he stopped at Mr. David Gould's, he had his horse. After leaving Mr. Gould's, he went towards home, it is supposed, (as a wallet which he carried with him, was found near his house,) but instead of turning into a pair of bars which led to his house, he turned outrectly back, passed Mr. Gould's house, and was found dead the next morning near the bars, where we now turn in to go to Sandy Shore. And what is very remarkable, his son was found dead the same day, in a clay pit in Medford.

Two ancient buildings formerly stood near where the house of E. H. Stearns now stands. About half a mile northeast from the house of said Stearns, an ancient building formerly stood occupied by a family named Howe. An old orchard near where the house stood, still retains the name of Howe orchard. About one-third of a mile west from this there formerly stood a house occupied by a family named Fensom. It was afterwards occupied by a man named Daniel Connery, who married one of the Fensom family. It was for a long time called Connery's den. What kind of beasts inhabited there, is not exactly known. One thing is pretty certain, however, which is, that the lion, rum, was one of the most ferocious among them.

I have now attempted to give an account of those buildings concerning which there is no date with regard to the time of their erection. I have also given some incidents connected with the inhabitants who lived in them.

This town was incorporated in the year 1725. The following is the Act of incorporation.

An Act for Dividing the Town of Charlestown, and Erecting a New Town there by the name of Stoneham.

WHEREAS the Northerly Part of the Town of Charlestown, within the County of Middlesex is competently filled with Inhabitants, who labor under great Difficulties by their Remoteness from the Place of Publick Worship, &c. And have thereupon made their Application to the said Town of Charlestown, and have likewise Addressed this Court that they may be set off a distinct and separate Town, and be Vested with all the Powers and Privileges of a Town, and the Inhabitants of Charlestown by their Agents having Consented to their being set off accordingly; And a Committee of this Court having Viewed the Northerly Part of the said Town of Charlestown, and reported in favor of the Petitioners:

Be it therefore Enacted by the Lieutenant Governour, Council and Representatives, in General Court Assembled, and by the Authority of the same, That the Northerly part of the said Town of Charlestown: That is to say, All the Lands lying on the East side of Woburn, the South side of Reading, the West side of Malden, and the North side of the

Fifth Range of the First Division of Charlestown Wood-lots, be and hereby is set off and constituted a separate Township by the name of Stoneham. And that the bounds and limits of the said town of Stoneham be according to the Agreement made in November, One thousand seven hundred and twenty-five, by and between the Committee or Agents for and in behalf of the said Town of Charlestown, and the Petitioners of the Northerly part thereof, wherein it was consented and agreed, That the Five Ranges or Remaining Part of the said first Division do remain to the Town of Charlestown, agreeable to a former Grant to the Town made in the year 1657–8. And that the Inhabitants of the Northerly half of Charlestown should have and enjoy that Tract of Land lying in the bounds aforesaid, commonly called and known by the Name of Gould's Farm, now under Lease to Messieurs Thomas and Daniel Gould, containing One hundred and ten Acres, or thereabouts: Also one-half of all the Town's Meadow (and Upland) lying on Spot Pond, both for Quantity and Quality, containing Seventy-nine Acres (by Capt. Burnap's Plat) as an Estate in Fee, with an equal Share in Spot Pond; the said Lands or the value thereof to be improved for the Settling and maintaining an Orthodox Minister, to dispense the Word and Ordinances among them: The Inhabitants of the said northerly half of Charlestown being by virtue of the said Agreement to be debarred from any Claims or Demands of and to any Lands, Money, Rents, or Incomes of what kind soever, which now are or shall belong to the Town of Charlestown, as well those several Farms and Land lying within the bounds abovesaid, as all other Estate or Income either Real or Personal, and from all Demands for Highways, that so the Town of Charlestown may quietly and peaceably enjoy the same: And further is it to be understood, That none of the Land contained in the two Ranges and half belonging to the first Division, shall on any pretence whatsoever be Assessed or Taxed by the said Town of Stoneham, except those Lands that shall be put under Improvement, such as Mowing, Plowing, and Pasturing.

And be it further Enacted by the Authority aforesaid, That the Inhabitants of the Northerly half of Charlestown, living within the bounds aforesaid, be and hereby are Vested with the Powers, Privileges and Immunities that the Inhabitants of any of the Towns of this Province by Law are or ought to be Vested with: And that the Inhabitants of the said Town of Stoneham do within the space of two Years from the Publication of this Act, Erect and Finish a suitable

19

House for the Public Worship of God, and as soon as may
be procure and settle a Learned, Orthodox Minister of good
Conversation, and make provision for his comfortable and
honorable Support; and likewise provide a School Master to
Instruct their Youth in Writing and Reading; and that
thereupon they be discharged from any Payments for the
Maintenance of the Ministry and School in the Town of
Charlestown.

Provided, That the Inhabitants of Stoneham, nevertheless
are to pay their respective proportion to two several
Assessments already made by the Assessors of Charlestown
for County and Town Charges; and David Gould, one of the
present Constables of Charlestown, is required to Collect and
Pay in such Parts and Proportions of each of said Assessments, as are committed to him by the said Assessors of
Charlestown, according to the Powers and Directions in the
Warrants duly made and delive'd; Anything in this Act to
the contrary notwithstanding.

This town I am told took its name from a town called
Stoneham in England. On Tuesday, March 22d, 1725, the
committee from the town of Charlestown, met a committee
chosen by this town and set the bounds as follows. Begin-
ning at Holden's line.

1st. A heap of stones, the west side of a little cedar.
2d. A heap of stones.
3d. A large red oak.
4th. A small tall white oak with a crotch.
5th. A tall walnut.
6th. A white oak with a crotch near the top.
7th. A young white oak with a crotch about half way up,
on the west side of a hill east from Spot Pond.
8th. A heap of stones near a small white oak, within
twelve rods of the east side of the pond.
9th. A tall walnut about twenty rods south of the pond.
10th. A dead white oak stump, about twelve rods west of
the pond, with a heap of stones about it.
11th. A red oak on the north side of a clift of rocks.
12th. A young walnut with a heap of stones about
twelve rods east of Turkey Swamp.
13th. A large red oak about six rods, near Turkey
Swamp.
14th. A heap of stones upon a flat rock about twenty rods
west of Turkey Swamp.
15th. A pine tree on a rocky hill.

16th. A heap of stones with a stake against a stone wall upon Woburn line.

The trees are marked on the south side with C, and on the north side with S. A true record of the bounds between Charlestown and Stoneham.

DANIEL GOULD, Town Clerk.

The town of Woburn was first settled in 1640. The bounds between this town and Reading were of a more definite character. Reading was also settled in 1640.

As certain lands were reserved by Charlestown in the act of incorporation, it may be well to state, that the farms of Caleb Wiley, widow Mirandi Richardson, and Ephraim Pierce, were included in the reserved portions of land. The town of Charlestown relinquished their title to these lands about forty years since.

The first public meeting held for business by this town was on December 24th, 1725. Timothy Belden, Sen., was chosen moderator, and Daniel Gould was chosen Town Clerk. At this meeting they voted to build a meeting house. For this purpose they chose a committee to examine the meeting house at Lynn End. The dimensions of the house were to be 36 feet in length and 32 feet in with. They however afterwards concluded to have it 40 feet in length and 36 feet in width, with 20 foot posts. The committee chosen to examine the meeting house at Lynn End were Jonathan Green, Daniel Gould, and Daniel Gould, Jr. The committee to prepare materials for building, consisted of Capt. John Vinton, Daniel Gould, Jr., and Lieutenant Timothy Wright. This committee were also instructed to procure the spot of land on which to set the meeting house; also a place to build a Parsonage, and likewise provide a burying ground. The first board of Selectmen, consisted of Capt. Benjamin Gerry, Capt. John Vinton, Peter Hay, Timothy Belden, and Lieutenant Timothy Wright. For many years five persons constituted the board of Selectmen. I am told however, that they served without any compensation. At a meeting held on the 16th day of March, 1726, they voted to raise £120 towards defraying the expense of building the meeting-house. It is said there was a good deal of contention with regard to the location of the house, some being very anxious to have it stand on the plain somewhere near the house of Reuben Locke. They however finally voted to have it stand between the black oak tree and the red oak tree upon the hill near the end of the school-house. It was raised about the last

of November, 1726. The following are some of the items
of expense connected with the raising of the meeting
house.

Paid for five gallons of rum, £1, 00s., 6d.
" " bread, 0, 12, 0.
" Capt. Gerry, for cider, 0, 15, 0.

The lime used in building was taken from the marble pit
now owned by Joseph Hurd, situated at the southwest part of
the town. There are two pits open at the present time. The
western pit is said to have been open from time immemorial.
The former practice of removing the marble to make lime, was
that of making a fire in the pit, thereby rendering it more
susceptible of impression from the tools made use of for removing
it. Marble of an excellent quality might still be obtained there were it not that the expense of getting it out would
outweigh its value when ready for use. This pit lies north
from what is now called Bear Hill. This was formerly called
Bears Hill, from the fact of its having been a noted place for
the residence of those animals. Gov. Winthrop states in his
history of Massachusetts, that he was travelling this way on
a certain occasion, and stopped upon Bears Hill, to rest and
refresh himself with food. On examining for his provisions it
seems his servant forgot to put up anything but some cheese.
from which circumstance he called Bear Hill Cheese Rock.
He also gave to Spot Pond its present name, from having so
many islands, rocks, &c., in it.

The town burying ground originally contained one-fourth
of an acre. It was afterwards enlarged to its present size,
which is about one acre. The land to enlarge it was pro-
cured of Mr. James Hay.

At a general town meeting held Oct. 14, 1754, the following
votes were passed:

Voted, That the town will seat the negroes in Stoneham,
in Stoneham meeting-house.

Voted, That the negro men in Stoneham shall set in the
hind seat in the side gallery, in the west end of Stoneham
meeting-house, and the negros' wives and other negro wo-
men shall set in the hind seat in the side gallery, in the east
end of said meeting-house, and nowhere else in said meeting-
house if there be convenient room in said seats, except it be
on special occasions.

The old road leading to Medford was built about the year 1731, at least that branch of it passing near the house of Joseph Hurd, a short distance east from Spot Pond. The road passing through what is called the meeting-house swamp, has also been built about one hundred years. A path formerly led over what is now called the old flat logs, about fifty rods south from the present causeway, leading through said meeting-house swamp. In 1760 they voted to choose a committee to meet with committees that might be chosen by the towns of Reading and Woburn, for the purpose of building a work-house for the benefit of said towns. What the result of their meeting was I have not ascertained, though the probability is, that they were not successful in their proposed union. They also about this time voted to raise the sum of £66 18s. and 4d., for the purpose of repairing the meeting-house. It was accordingly newly shingled, new windows put in, &c.

It was customary at that time when children were taken into a family to be brought up, (or even to remain a few months,) to give notice of the same to the Selectmen. The following is a copy of the same: "Gentlemen, Selectmen, of the town of Stoneham, these lines are to inform or notify you, that I have this day taken into my house one Catherine Olentick to live with me for her work; she is about twelve years old. As to her circumstances, she has a father to take care of her." Notices of this kind seem to have been given, in order that the town might be apprised of the fact, that they might possibly have accession to the list of paupers, from time to time, as the case might be. It was also customary when an individual came into town to live, to warn them to leave in so many days. It seems a law of this kind was framed so that each town might be on their guard, as it respected paupers.

The following is a copy of a record of this kind: Stoneham, Nov. 20th, 1772. Ebenezer Richardson was warned out of Stoneham, and the place he came from was Boston. And the persons hereafter mentioned, Ebenezer Williams and his wife Elizabeth and their son Ebenezer. The place from whence they came last is Reading. It is understood that if they were natives of Reading, it would belong to Reading to support them. If they were not natives of Reading, and Reading neglected to warn them out, they would still have them to maintain in case they became paupers. But if Reading had warned them out, they would have no difficulty whatever with regard to the case.

At a meeting held on the first day of November, 1774, the following patriotic resolves were passed. The preamble reads thus:

We the inhabitants of the town of Stoneham being legally assembled, sincerely declare our strict attachment to the Constitution of our nation; and our unfeigned loyalty to our Rightful Lord and Sovereign King, George the Third; ardently wishing that we might ever live in the utmost harmony with Great Britain. Yet we are driven to the disagreeable necessity to say; that having taken into serious consideration the precarious state of the liberties of North America, and more especially the present distressed condition of this insulted Province, embarrassed as it is by several acts of the British Parliamentary vending, as we apprehend to the entire subversion of our natural and charter rights, among which is the act of blocking up the harbor of Boston; therefore we do solemnly covenant and engage with each other:

1st. That we will henceforth suspend all commercial intercourse with Great Britan until they shall afford us relief.

2d. That we will not buy, purchase, or consume any goods or merchandize, which shall arrive in America from Great Britain, from and after the last day of September ensuing.

These things we solemnly promise to observe, provided, no better scheme shall be devised to answer the same end, by the Congress, who are to meet at Philadelphia to consult the general political interests of America.

The town held another meeting subsequent to the meeting of Congress, when they voted to accept the doings of said Congress in all respects.

I have before stated that the house of Dea. Ebenezer Bucknam was the place of rendezvous, during the time of the Revolution. I am told the town voted on a certain occasion that no gun should be discharged in town, except under the following rule: a certain number were chosen as minute men. The first person that received an alarm was immediately with two or more individuals to repair to the common, front of the old meeting house. The discharge of the muskets in succession was considered as a general alarm, when the members of the company were immediately to repair to the place of rendezvous. The company in this town were called out at the time of the battle of Lexington. It will be remembered Samuel Sprague was commander of the company. He however previous to reaching Lexington told the members of the company, that

their numbers were so small that he thought it would be well
to separate and each one look out for himself. They accordingly separated into companies of three or four, and scatter-
ed themselves abroad. Edward Bucknam, Timothy Matthews, and James Willey went in company together. Somewhere in the vicinity of Lexington they were discovered by
some British Regulars. A bullet passed between the left
ear and skull of Bucknam, also through the hats of both
Matthews and Willey. Thus did our fathers expose their
health and lives that we might enjoy the blessings of civil
and religious liberty.

It will be remembered that while speaking of the several
buildings and their inhabitants, I spoke of a family by the
name of Connery. After his decease, in the year 1776, a part
or all of his family came upon the town. The following is the
copy of an indenture by which the Selectmen of the town
bound out Abigail Connery.

This Indenture Witnesseth, That, Samuel Sprague, Gentleman, and Timothy Taylor Daniel Gould Jun'r. Timothy Wright Jun'r. and Peter Hay Jun'r.
yeomen, all of the town of Stoneham in the County of middlesex and province of the massachusetts Bay in New-England and Selectmen of Said town
So far forth as our power doth will or may Extend as Selectmen, by and with
the assent of two Justices of the Peace in said County Have (agreeable to the
trust by Law to us Committed) put and Bound and by these presents Do put
place and Bind Abigail Connery (Daughter of Daniel Connery Deceased) a
poor Garl Belonging to Said town apprintice to Jonathan Green of the town
of Stoneham, aforesaid Gentleman, and his wife to Learn to Spin net and
Sow and with him the said Johnathan Green and his wife after the manner of
an apprentice to Serve from the Day of the Date hereof for and Dureing the
term of ten years Eleven months and twenty-seven Days (until she comes to
the age of Eighteen years) to be Compleat and Ended during all which
Said term the Said apprentice her said master and mistress faithfully shall
Serve their Secrets keep and Lawful Commands Gladly Every where Obey
she shall Do no Damage to her Said master or mistress nor see it to be done
by others without Letting or Giveing notice thereof to her said master or
mistress She Shall not waiste her said masters or mistresses Goods nor
Lend them to any She shall not Commit fornification, nor contract matri-
mony within said term. at Cards dice or other unlawfull Game She shall
not play Whereby her said master or mistress may have Damage with their
Goods nor the Goods of others She shall not absent her Self by Day or by
night from her said masters or mistresses Service, without their Leave nor
haunt ale houses taverns or play houses but in all things behave herself as
a faithful apprentice ought to Do towards her said master and mistress
Dureing said term of ten years Eleven months and twenty seven days (until she comes to the age of Eighteen years) and the said Jonathan Green for
himself and his wife doth hereby Covenant and promise to teach and Instruct or cause to be taught and instructed in the art or traid of Spinning
netting and Sowing (common work) by proper ways or means (if the said
apprentice be capable to Learn) finding unto said apprentice Good and
Sufficient meat Drink washing and Lodging both in Sickness and helth
Dureing said term. and at the Expiration thereof to Give unto the said apprentice two Suits of apparrel both wooling and Linning fitting for all
parts of her Body one of Said Suits fitting and proper for Lords Days and
the other of Said Suits fitting and Suteable for common and working Days
Suteable for such an apprentice and also [within Said term teach her the

said apprentice to Read In Testimony whereof the parties to these presents have hereunto Interchaugeably Set their hands and Seals the Sixth Day of may in the Sixteenth year of his majesties's Reign, annoque Domini one thousand Seven hundred and Seventy Six.

Signed Sealed and Delivered }
in presence of us

DAVID GREEN
JONATHAN GREEN Jun'r

SAMUEL SPRAGUE
TIMOTHY TAYLER
TIMOTHY WRIGHT, Junr.
PETER HAY Jun'r

Middlesex: ss: May 6: 1776.—We the subscribers, two of the Justices of the Peace, Do alow of and consent to the binding out of the said Abigail Cosery to the said Jonathan Green.
(Signed)   DAVID GREEN, THAD'S MASON, Justices of Peace.

With many of the transactions of our grandfathers and great grandfathers we are much amused. On one occasion they voted at a town meeting that it was not expedient to make use of a bass viol during singing on the Sabbath. The reason for such an act was, that the bass viol was a species of fiddle, and as the fiddle or violin was made use of at balls and parties it was therefore argued to be wrong to use the bass viol on the Sababth.

I proceed now to give an account of the various buildings which have been put up at different times, or rather to state when they were put up. This statement includes all the buildings in town with the exception of those before mentioned. The earliest date of the erection of a dwelling house is that of the house occupied by Dea. David and Zacheous Gerry, which it is supposed was built in the year 1708, as a brick having this date upon it was taken from a jamb of one of the fireplaces about forty years since. In 1747 the house owned and occupied by the Rev. John H. Stevens, was built for the use of Rev. Mr. Carnes, second minister in this town. In the year 1756, the house of Capt. John H. Wright, and the old house torn down by Allen Rowe, a few years since, were both built. Both are said to have been raised in one day. A large concourse of people were present to witness the raising of the buildings. In 1781 one house was built; in 1792, 1; in 1795, 1; in 1799, 1; in 1802, 1; in 1804, 1; in 1806, 2; in 1807, 2; in 1809, 2; in 1812, 4; in 1813, 1; in 1816, 4; in 1817, Mr. Robert Barnes built the house now occupied by Richard R. Barnes. His work at the commencement was nearly as laborious as that of the first settlers; having to perform the hard labor of cutting and removing trees, stumps, &c. He lived but a few years to enjoy the fruit of his labors. In 1819, 3 houses were built. In 1820,1; in 1821, 3; in 1822, 2; in 1823, 2; in 1825, 1; in 1826, 1; in 1827, 1; in 1828, 2; in 1829, 3; in 1830, 3; in 1831, 4; in 1832, 2; in 1833, 2; in 1834, 4; in 1835, 2; in 1836, 10; in 1837, 5; in

1838, 5; in 1839, 3; in 1840, 7; in 1841, 8; in 1842, 5; in 1843, up to August 1st, but 1.

The number of dwelling-houses that have been built in town since its settlement is about 200. At present the number is 160. If I include several shops which have been fitted up for dwelling-houses, it makes the number about 170.

Previous to building the Andover and Medford turnpike for about 60 years, from 60 to 70 buildings were all that stood in town, and the population varied but little if any during that period of time.

There have been 11 school-houses built at different times. The town house was built in 1826, and moved to where it now stands in 1833.

The first meeting house, it will be remembered, was built in 1726. I find no record of any dedication services, though no   bt there were appropriate services when they first assembled in it for public worship. The meeting house which was destroyed by fire on Sunday, Jan. 5th, 1840, was raised on Wednesday and Thursday, the 29th and 30th days of June, 1803. It was completed and dedicated on the 14th day of December following. The exercises on the occasion were as follows: The Rev. Mr. Reynolds of Wilmington made the first prayer. The Rev. Mr. Sanborn, of Reading, made the dedicatory prayer; the Rev. Mr. Stevens, pastor, preached the sermon, from Haggai, 2d chap., 7th verse: "I will fill this house with glory." The Sabbath previous to this, Mr. Stevens preached a farewell sermon to the old meeting house, and the day after the dedication of the new house, the people assembled together and took it down; it having been the place for the public worship of God, for 77 years. In 1840 two neat and commodious meeting houses were erected, viz: one Congregational and one Universalist; both being completed and dedicated the same year.

The Universalist meeting house was dedicated August 20th. The order of exercises was as follows:—Reading select Scriptures by Rev. J. G. Adams, of Malden; Introductory Prayer, by Rev. J. C. Waldo, of Woburn; Dedicatory Prayer by Rev. Hosea Ballou, 2d, of Medford. Sermon by Rev. Abel C. Thomas of Lowell; Address to the Society, by Rev. Thomas Whittemore, of Cambridgeport. The church connected with the Universalist Society, at present consists of 31 members. Present acting Pastor, Rev. Woodbury M. Fernald. The Congregational meeting house was dedicated Oct. 22d. A sermon was preached on the occasion by the Rev. Edward Cleveland, acting pastor;

dedicatory prayer by Rev. Mr. Emerson, of South Reading.

The Rev. James Osgood was the first pastor of the church and society in this town. He was ordained Sept. 10th, 1729. The following ministers assisted in his ordination, viz: Rev. Richard Brown, of the 1st church, Reading; Rev. Samuel Fiske, of the 1st church, Salem; Rev. Hall Abbott, of Charlestown; Rev. Benj. Prescott, of the 3d church, Salem; Rev. Joseph Emerson of Malden; Rev. Daniel Putnam of the 2d church, Reading. The church was organized a short time previous to Mr. Osgood's ordination; and consisted of 13 members, viz: Ephraim Larrabee, Abraham Gould, Jacob Howe, Edward Bucknam, Joseph Bryant, Jonathan Griffin, David Gould, Daniel Gould, Jr., Samuel Sprague, Ebenezer Knight, Ebenezer Parker, Thomas Cutler, and David Gould.

Mr. Osgood died suddenly, March 2d, 1745. His wife afterward married Capt. Ralph Hart, of Boston, but died in this town, August 11th, 1801, being 83 years of age. She is said to have been a very amiable and excellent person.

The second minister was Rev. Mr. John Carnes, of Boston, who was settled, Dec. 17th, 1747. The order of exercises was as follows: Rev. Mr. Elliot, of Boston, made the introductory prayer; Rev. Mr. Prentice, of Charlestown, preached the sermon; Rev. Mr. Emerson, of Malden, gave the charge; and Rev. Mr. Hobby, of Reading, gave the right hand of fellowship.

It was customary in those days for the minister to read the psalm to be sung, as is the practice at the present time. After reading the psalm it devolved on one of the deacons of the church to deal it out to the singers, a line or two at a time. On one occasion, after the psalm had been read, the good deacon took the book and commenced dealing out the hymn; it read as follows:

"Spikenard, saffron, calamus, and cinnamon also,
 All incensed trees with aloes,
 And all chief spices grow, &c.

The deacon very soon found himself entangled among so many spices, and the minister rose to help him along through the first line. The deacon again rose, but again the minister was under the necessity of rising to help him along. When the deacon made the third trial he could not get through with the line. The minister then arose and said to him, "Deacon, you can't read." It should however be borne in mind, that people at that time could not generally read so well as at the present time. The advantages for education were then small.

Mr. Carnes was dismissed July 31st, 1757.

The Rev. John Searle was installed Jan. 17th, 1758. The order of exercises was as follows: introductory prayer by Rev. Mr. Parsons, of Newburyport; sermon by Rev. Mr. Emerson, of Malden; charge by Rev. Mr. Cook, of Cambridge; right hand of fellowship by Rev. Mr. Robie, of Lynn; concluding prayer by Rev. Mr. Sherman, of Woburn.

Mr. Searle was dismissed April 24th, 1776.

Rev. John Cleavland was settled Oct. 19th, 1785. The order of exercises was as follows: introductory prayer by Rev. Mr. Bradford, of Rowley; Sermon by Rev. Mr. Cleavland, father of the pastor elect; Charge by Rev. Mr. Hopkins, of Salem; Right Hand of Fellowship by Rev. Rr. Bresh, of Topsfield.

Mr. Cleavland was dismissed Oct. 23d, 1794.

Rev. John H. Stevens was settled Nov. 11th, 1795. The order of exercises was as follows: Introductory Prayer by Rev. Mr. Spaulding of Salem; Sermon by Rev. Mr. Bradford, of Rowley; Consecrating Prayer by Rev. Mr. Litchfield, of Carlisle; Charge by Rev. Mr. Prentice, of South Reading; Concluding Prayer by Rev. Mr. Aiken, of Dracut.

Mr. Stevens was dismissed Nov. 11th, 1827, having been minister in this town for 32 years,

Rev. Joseph Searle was settled May 1st, 1838. The order of exercises was as follows: Introductory Prayer by Rev. Brown Emerson, of Salem; Sermon by Rev. Dr. Fay, of Charlestown; Installing Prayer by Rev. Reuben Emerson, of South Reading; Charge by Rev. Dr. Beecher, of Boston; Address to the church and people by Rev. Samuel Green, of Boston; Right Hand of Fellowship by Rev. Mr. Bennett, of Woburn; Concluding Prayer by Rev. Mr. Warner, of Medford.

Mr. Searle was dismissed Jan. 2d, 1832.

Rev. Jonas Colburn was settled Aug. 1st, 1832. The order of exercises was as follows: Introductory Prayer, by Rev. Mr. Warner, of Medford; Sermon by Rev. Mr. Emerson, of South Reading; Charge by Rev. Mr. Stevens, of Haverhill, formerly pastor of the church; Installing Prayer by Rev. Mr. Reynolds of Wilmington; Right Hand of Fellowship by Rev. Mr. Bennett, of Woburn; Concluding Prayer by Rev. Mr. Reid, of Reading.

Mr. Colburn was dismissed Feb. 27th, 1837.

The present pastor, Rev. John Haven, was installed Feb-

24th, 1841. The order of exercises was as follows: Introductory Prayer by Rev. H. S. Green of Lynnfield; Sermon by Rev. H. Winslow, of Boston; Installing Prayer by Rev. Mr. Emerson, of South Reading; Charge by Rev. B. Smith, of Rye, N. H.; Right Hand of Fellowship by Rev. Mr. Bennett, of Woburn; Concluding Prayer by Rev. Mr. Baker, of Medford.

The church at present consists of 120 members.

The first marriage attended by Rev. Mr. Osgood, was that of John Tidd, of Woburn, to Abigail Gould, of Stoneham. This was Nov. 26th, 1729.

In the year 1737, Jan. 11th, I find the following marriage; Sambo, of Stoneham, married to Mercar, of Malden. The same year, Nov. 28th, Mingo, married to Moll, negro servants of Peter Hay, Jr.

In 1743, one hundred years ago, I find the following; Obadiah How, negro servant of Mr. Souther, married to Priscilla Pomp, both of Stoneham.

According to the record kept by Mr. Osgood, he attended 44 marriage ceremonies during his ministry.

I find no record kept by either of the three succeeding ministers, Carnes, Searle, or Cleaveland.

According to the record kept by Rev. Mr. Stevens, I find that during his ministry he solemnized 175 marriages. Mr. Stevens also recorded 448 births.

With regard to the deaths no definite statement can be made. Up to the time of Mr. Stevens's settlement no regular record was kept. In passing through the burying ground I find something like 90 grave stones erected previous to that time; or the deaths occurred previously. But as it was formerly difficult and expensive to obtain grave stones, the probabliity is that very few had stones erected.

The following is a record of the deaths, as kept by Rev. Mr. Stevens:—In 1795 there were 5 deaths; in 1796, 4; in 1797, 9; in 1798, 5; in 1799, 9; in 1800, 10; in 1801, 8; in 1802, 6; in 1803, 11; in 1804, 6; in 1805, 14; in 1806, 4; in 1807, 8; in 1808, 5; in 1809, 5; in 1810, 8; in 1811, 10; in 1812, 3; in 1813, 11; in 1814, 6; in 1815, 8; in 1816, 8; in 1817, 16; in 1818, 4; in 1819, 6; in 1820, 5; in 1821, 4; in 1822, 5; in 1823, 8; in 1824, 11; in 1825, 14; in 1826, 12; in 1827, 9. The remaining account I take from the record of the sexton:— In 1828, 16; in 1829, 5; in 1830, 5; in 1831, 16; in 1832, 14; in 1833, 16; in 1834, 16; in 1835, 7; in 1836, 20; in 1837, 18; in 1838, 7; in 1839, 19; in 1840, 9; in 1841, 14; in 1842, 10; in 1843, up to August 1st, 12.

It will be perceived that 1836 was the most mortal of any year, 20 be'ng removed by death.

I ought to have stated previously, that in the year 1813, two Indians, of the Penobscot tribe, came into town and took up their abode a few rods south from Mr. Hurd's old factory. They employed themselves in making baskets. It seems that, like most people of that time, they were in the habit of drinking intoxicating liquors. It was stated that they insulted the workmen connected with Odiorne's nail factory in Malden. On a certain night some individuals approached their hut and discharged several guns loaded with bullets, nails, &c. The Indians were both wounded. The man died and was interred in the burying-yard in this town. It was supposed by many that his body was taken for the purpose of dissection. This was proved to be the fact, several years after, when the grave was opened. The coffin remained, but the body was gone. Another body was interred in the same grave, which was also taken away.

It appears from the record kept of the deaths, that between 500 a'd 600 have, in the space of a few year., gone down to the grave. The probability is, that a number nearly or quite equal to the present population of the town ow lie in the burying-ground. The earliest date upon any grave-stone is that of Lieut. Timothy Wright, who died in 1728.

The Scollays, the Southers, the Bucks, together with the slaves formerly kept in town, Kingstone, Cato, Simon, Obadiah, and many others, have no grave-stones to show us where they lie. I am told, however, that the negro servants were buried on the east side of the yard. But as their bodies have returned to their native dust, and as the coffins have decayed, the sods which covered their graves have settled down to their former level.

Thus I have attempted to give a brief history of this town, though I am aware it is a very imperfect account, compared with what it might have been, had it been attended to several ye°rs since.

The following description may at present be given of this town:

This is a small town, rocky and uneven. It has some good soil, and a considerable quantity of wood-land. It was incorporated in 1725. The population in 1837 was 932; present population about 1050. During the year ending April 1st, 1837, there were made in this town 380,100 pairs of shoes, valued at $184,717, employing more than half its inhabitants. Spot Pond, a beautiful sheet of soft and pure water, lies in this town, 8 miles north from Boston. It covers an area of 283 acres, and is 143 feet above high water mark at Boston. There is also said to be a fall of 100 feet in the distance of about 100 rods from the pond. For many years, many of the inhabitants of the city of Boston have been anxious to take the water from this pond to the city, by means of aqueducts. They are about commencing operations to that effect.

In looking back to our ancestors and their descendants, we find that four generations have followed the first settlers of this town, in rapid succession, to the house appointed for all the living. But, while the wheels of time are rolling on, and carrying generation after generation to the grave, the immortal part of man is in its infancy. The soul is destined to survive the wreck of nature and the crush of worlds.

> "Behold how soon the year is past and gone!
> For time like streams is ever rolling on;
> The rose is fragrant, but it fades in time,
> The violet sweet, but quickly past the prime;
> White lilies hang their heads and soon decay,
> And whiter snows in minutes melt away.
>   Such and so withering is our blooming youth.
> To things immortal time can do no wrong,
> And that which never is to die forever must be young."

On Friday evening, Nov. 25th, 1819, one of the most brutal murders, anywhere on record, was committed in this town. I refer to the murder of Jacob Gould. The following account, published by Rev. J. W. Poland, a native of Stoneham, I copy principally from the Farmers Monthly Visitor of March, 1843, printed at Concord, N. H.

THE STONEHAM MURDER.

Among the early settlers of Stoneham, Mass., there were some by the name of Gould. The name has now become quite common in that town, and in the adjoining town of South Reading. There were two families of that name settled near to Spot pond, on the old road leading to Malden and Medford. One of the families, at the time in which the murder took place, consisted of two brothers, who were bachelors, a sister, who was a maiden lady, and a widow Winship, hired help. The names of the brothers were Jacob and David; and the sister's name was Polly. Jacob was the oldest, and owned the real estate; but the property of David and

Polly was chiefly in money. Sometimes they would let money, where there was good security, but generally preferred to keep it in specie. It was generally understood among the people that there was considerable specie in that house, and many a thief, no doubt, had longed to get hold of it. At length the time came for the hoarded gold and silver to get into circulation.

A man by the name of Dalton, who had formerly resided in Stoneham, was an inmate of the State prison at Charlestown, Mass., when the murder took place. It was ascertained afterwards, that this Dalton informed some convicts, who were about graduating, of this store of money, and instructed them how to get it. (At that time there were opportunities for the convicts to converse with each other.) The name of one of these was Daniels, who had formerly been a shoe dealer in Boston. A few days before this murder, Daniels passed through that part of the town in which the Goulds lived, on a tour of discovery. He made inquiries of two boys, whom he met separately, relative to the condition of the family; "whether they had money; had they guns, or dogs, or were they pretty courageous?" The boys' answers probably satisfied him that there could be little difficulty in the way of making an effort to get hold of the money.

The widow who lived with this family was knowing to their having a considerable sum of money, as she had heard them talk about it, and by some was supposed to have been accessory to the robbery.

On the 25th of November, 1819, Jacob went up to town to get some rum, as he was intending to kill his hogs the next day. Poor man! he little thought of being butchered himself. He had come home, and between eight and nine o'clock, while he sat drinking some sling, in rushed three ruffians with their faces blacked, and with dirks in hand, and demanded his money. Jacob attempted to defend himself with his chair, but they overpowered him. He fell, being stabbed in several places; and one of the wounds, which reached the region of the heart, proved mortal. David, through fright, passed by an axe which stood near him, and which had been newly ground, and while in the act of taking up a billet of wood, felt the prick of a dagger. On turning round he received two wounds; one in his side, or abdomen, and one against his heart, but which was prevented from reaching it by the dirk's passing through the thick part of his left arm first. As no further resistance was made, the robbers pro-

33

ceeded to bind the hands of David and Polly, which they
tied so tight as to cause the cords to cut into the flesh. The
fourth man stood at the door to keep watch, and to prevent
escape, and was supposed by some to have been a man who
formerly resided in town, by the name of Clifton. After
their hands were secured, they were taken up stairs one at a
time to hand over their money. Jacob was carried up first.
It seems he at that time had but one $5 bill. This he had
reserved for Benjamin Lynde, of Malden, who a short time
previous had his house destroyed by fire.

After Jacob was taken down stairs, David was led up: he
had about $200. Afterwards Polly was compelled to go and
get her money. She had $600, in six deerskin bags of $100
each, deposited in Jacob's chest.

In going up the stairs, the light went out in the dark lan-
tern which they had with them, and in the scuffle to secure
their prisoner, Polly's hands were badly cut with a knife, as
well as one of the fingers of a robber. This robber was evidently Daniels, who was afterwards detected, partly by means
of this wound. After they had secured the money they
threw the poor creatures down cellar, and set a table against
the door. The widow walked down among the rest. They
then drank upon the rum, divided the money, and finally left.
telling them that they were going to a near neighbor's (David Gould's) to serve them the same; also stating that they
should leave one to guard them for the space of two hours.
when they could come up if they saw fit after that time. At
their request, they threw down a feather bed for them to lie
upon.

But Jacob's dying groans aroused the feelings of David.
and at about eleven o'clock he ventured to go up; went to a
neighbor's and gave the alarm. Three men started out immediately with their guns, and went to the house with him.
The robbers had probably been gone two hours.

By daylight the whole town was aroused, and many were,
in pursuit. Jacob died about three o'clock in the morning.

Though the most diligent search was made, nothing of the
robbers could be found. A reward of five hundred dollars
was offered by David Gould for the detection of the robbers,
and the Governor of the State added five hundred more.
This started out many in pursuit. It was not long before
Daniels (the man spoken of before) was taken up in New-
port, Rhode Island. There were many suspicious things
about him, all the particulars of which are not now recol-
lected. He had a cut on one of his fingers, which looked as

though it were done with a knife, but which he declared was caused by a sea-shell, while he was skipping it upon the water. There was blood in his pocket-book, and on some money, which he said came there by his putting in his finger after a rag to wrap around it. He had also some gold pieces, resembling those which had been described by the Goulds, but which he said he had taken in Boston, or somewhere else. The suspicions were so strong against him, that he was brought on to the jail at Lechmere Point, in Cambridge, and committed for trial. The two boys with whom the conversation had been held previous to the murder, were carried to the court-house and were required to go into a crowd of men, among whom was Daniels, and see if they could find the man who had conversed with them. One went in and immediately pointed out Daniels as the man. Daniels did not seem to be moved by this boy's story. The boy was then taken to another room, and the other boy brought in. He quickly walked up to Daniels and declared him to be the man, at the same time telling him what he said to him at the time mentioned. Daniels then turned pale, and began to sweat profusely. He did not have his trial in full at that time, and was again committed. Just before his trial was to take place, he hung himself in his cell, thereby confirming his guilt, though he made no confession.

About this time a man by the name of Phillips was taken up on suspicion of being concerned in this murder. He was at a gambling house in West Boston, and had money in his possession which answered to the description given of that lost in the robbery. Upon his examination, though David an Polly felt positive that the money was theirs, yet they did not dare to swear to it, and so he escaped. He left the State prison about the time Daniels did, and was no doubt an accomplice with him.

After this, another man was taken up at Portland, Me., but he was probably innocent. He was not retained.

It is now twenty-three years since this horrid transaction took place, and nothing further has been ascertained in relation to the r bbers.

The family are now all dead. David died July 6th, 1834; being in the 71st year of his age. Polly died Nov. 21st, 1836, being in the 78th year of her age; and the widow Winship died but a few years since at the almshouse in Medford.

Possibly the murderers are all dead.

CPSIA information can be obtained
at www.ICGtesting.com
Printed in the USA
395757LV00001B/2